Bending The Blues

By David Harp

D0117546

Copyright © musical i press, inc.
P.O. Box 1561
Montpelier, Vermont 05602
ISBN 0 - 918321 - 11 - 5

Book design by Rita Ricketson
Drawings by Don Mayne
Cover Photography by Jay Graham
Hands by David Harp

Distributed by Music Sales Corporation
225 Park Ave. South
New York, NY 10013

Printed in the United States of America by
Vicks Lithographic and Printing Corporation

Dedicated
To all the great benders of the past,
and to Barrie, Dave Mac, Joey
and the rest of the fun folk at
Music Sales Corp.

musical i press
Montpelier, Vermont

Contents

Please Read This First!

Before I even introduce myself, or start to explain bending, I'd like to talk about how to use this book and the tape that is available to accompany it. So — **Please Read This First** — it will help you to get the most out of *Bending The Blues*!

Who Can Use This Book?

I've tried to organize this book so that it can be used by *any* level of harmonica player, no matter whether you're a total beginner, or an intermediate, or an advanced harpist. But depending on how well you can already play, you may want to use this book in different ways. So I'd like to tell you exactly how to do that, right up front.

For Beginners

If you can't bend at all yet, you should probably begin at the beginning, and hey, that's where you are right now! Just keep on reading each section and trying each exercise as you go. Make sure that you don't get hung up or stuck on any of the early sections or exercises, even if they seem hard (they probably won't, except maybe for the one on Single Notes). I'll be trying a couple of different ways of explaining beginning bending, since I've learned that different people "get" bending in different ways. So just keep on reading the sections and trying the exercises, right up to page 58, because at least one of the ways is sure to work for you!

Maybe you wonder, "Why not just start wailing, and forget this reading and exercise stuff?" Well, bending takes a certain amount of preparation. I know that there is a lot of material to go through before we get to the actual bending, but I promise you that it will all help you to be a really good bender, in the long run. So be patient, and at least skim the entire beginner's part of the book — because trying to bend without understanding the whats, whys, and hows is like trying to run before you can walk!

I know that I go into too much beginning detail for a few of you, but I also know from my teaching career that many others of you will enjoy (and use) it all. But if you're really impatient, just read up to the **For Beginners Who Can't Wait** section on page

10, and I'll give you a shortcut. And, if you like, skip or skim the last two parts of this section, since they're aimed at people who can already bend (or think that they can!).

For People "Who Can Bend A Little"

In the classes and private lessons that I teach, I meet a lot of harp players who tell me they've taught themselves to bend "a little". Often, they don't really know if they can bend, or not. Some can actually bend pretty well, while a few others are mostly using what I call "The Pre-Bending Effect" (which I describe on page 22).

If you're really not sure how well you can bend, try this simple test. If you are really sure you can bend some, forget the test and just read the last paragraph in this section.

The Bend Test: Play the note 6 Blow, then play 5 Draw. Do it a few times. (If you can't get single notes well enough to do that, you're sure to have problems bending, and you'd better read the whole first part of the book.) Now play a 2 Draw, then bend it down. The 6 Blow and 2 Draw should sound pretty much the same, except that the 6 is higher by "one octave" (but don't worry about what an octave is, since I'll cover that later). Likewise, the 5 Draw and the note you get from bending the 2 Draw should sound similar. If they don't, you are not getting a complete bend, and you should probably at least skim the first part of the book.

6	**5**	**=**	**2**	**2**
Blow	*Draw*		*Draw*	*Draw bend*

If the 2 Draw Bent note and the 5 Draw sounded more or less the same, you can bend! Read the section on **My Notation System**, then go directly to page 48, and begin to sharpen your bending skills for the "Bent Major Scale" and Blues Scales. Or else turn to the section on any specific bend that you would like to work on. Of course, feel free to read as many of the sections between here and there, if you like, especially the **bold** ones or the ones marked by "bullet" dots like •. You just might learn something new!

For Serious Benders

If you're reading this sub-section, I'll take your word for it — you can probably bend, all right (but if you want a quickie test, take the one in the two paragraphs above)! So now it's up to you read the section on **My Notation System**, then to look at the "Degrees Of Bending" chart on page 9, and the Chromatic Scales on page 63, and see whether you can really hit every note. Can you use the High End Blow Bends? If not, check out page 58. Are you good at getting all three bent notes out of your 3 Draw hole? How about those jazzy Middle Blow Bends, 4, 5, and 6? They're tricky — better look at page 61. Or maybe some of my Scales and licks will be news to you!

About The Bending Tape

Perhaps this section should be entitled "Can I Really Learn To Bend By Reading About It". And the answer is: maybe. Some people seem to learn better by reading, others by listening. In any event, I've recorded a 90 minute cassette to illustrate most of the information in this book. So if you think that *listening* while you read might help you to understand the material better, you'll find the details on ordering on page 64.

Why I Wrote This Book

Basically, I wrote this book because I wish that I had had one like it when I started to play the harmonica twenty years ago.

Back in the late 1960's, I could hear the screaming, wailing sound of my favorite blues and rock harpists. But all I could pick out were single note melodies like *Oh When The Saints Go Marchin' In* and *Blowing In The Wind*. Great songs, but no punch to 'em, the way I played.

I'd go up to professional harp players who were taking a break between sets, and ask them what to do. That's how I found out that a technique known as bending made all the difference. But their instructions to me ("Just bend it, man, ya know?" or "Pull that note down with your mouth") didn't make much sense...

It took me over eight years of serious work — listening, taking lessons, studying music theory, and lots of just plain trial and error — before I even discovered all of the possible bends. Then it took me years of full-time harmonica teaching to learn the best ways to teach bending techniques to my beginning, intermediate, and advanced students.

In this book, I'll teach you everything that I now know about bending, and wish that someone had taught *me* back in 1969. I really believe that a book like this would have cut many years off the time it took me to reach a professional level of harp playing. With practice on your part, it can do the same for you. Enjoy!

Back To The Basics: Why We NEED To Bend

As I said on the cover, bending is *the* most important harmonica technique. It is absolutely crucial for blues, rock, country and jazz harp players, and extremely useful for folk, pop and classical fans as well . I'm going to take a minute to tell you exactly why that is, right now. I'll go into *much* more detail on all of this later on in the book.

What Exactly Is Bending?

Bending is the ability to change the highness or lowness of a harmonica note by changing the position of your tongue in your mouth.

That's what bending is. But in order to explain *how* bending happens, I'll have to talk a little bit about the insides of your harmonica, about sound, and about your tongue.

About Reeds

You probably know this already: that harmonicas are made so that each hole produces one note on the out breath, and a different note on the in breath. Each note is produced by forcing air over a thin piece of metal called a *reed*. One reed (the Blow note reed) is set in the top of each hole, and one reed (the Draw note reed) is set in the bottom of each hole.

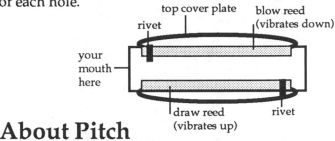

About Pitch

If you really want to know much about sound and music theory, you'll need to read one of my other books (please see page 64). But for bending purposes, this is all that you need to know:

The highness or lowness of any note is called the *pitch* of that note. All sound is caused by vibration. When something vibrates quickly (like a mosquito's wing), it produces a high-pitched sound. When something vibrates slowly (like a Harley Davidson's muffler), it produces a low-pitched sound.

The bigger a reed is, the slower it vibrates, and the lower the sound it makes is. The smaller a reed is, the faster it vibrates, and the higher the sound it makes is. So the reeds in the low end of your harp, like the number 1 and 2 holes, are much bigger than the reeds in the high end. And those bigger reeds vibrate slower, and sound lower, because:

The slower the speed of vibration, the lower the sound.

So How Do I Bend?

When your tongue is in a relaxed position, the group of muscles that make up your tongue are loose, and it just lays there in the bottom of your mouth. When you inhale or exhale through any hole of your harmonica with your tongue like this, the air flows smoothly — through the reed, and then right over your tongue.

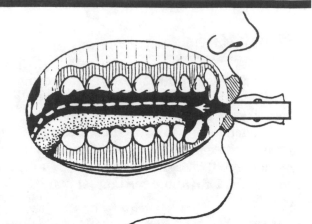

If you tense your tongue muscles so that your tongue "humps" up in a particular way, you can make the air stream hit your tongue, which changes the air flow. This change in air flow causes the reed to make a bigger back and forth movement than it usually does, which also causes the reed to vibrate slower than it normally does. And — big surprise — slowing down the speed of vibration of the reed makes the note sound lower. And there's your bend — a new note, completely different from the unbent note that you started with!

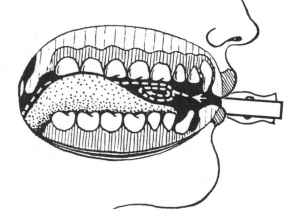

You can demonstrate this for yourself (without bending) like this: Hold your arm out straight at shoulder height. Move your hand up and down a distance of about six inches, as fast as you can. Now move your hand up and down a distance of about two feet, as fast as you can. Which can you do faster? Same thing happens to the reed — when the changed air flow forces it to move further, it just can't move (vibrate) as fast, and so the pitch gets lower...

Sounds pretty simple so far, doesn't it? Just hump up your tongue a bit, and bend the note. But there's more to it than that. For instance, some reeds can produce one bent note, and other reeds can produce up to three different bends. And, unfortunately, bending each reed on each key harmonica requires a different tongue position. So that's what the rest of this book is gonna be about!

Why Bending Is Essential

Now that I've given you the *how* of bending, here's the *why* of it. Bending is essential because it allows us to play extra notes that were not "built in" to the harmonica. How many extra notes? Well, check out your standard ten hole harmonica (sometimes called a "diatonic", or "Major Scale", or "Blues" style harmonica). It has ten holes with two reeds in each hole, so it should be able to play 20 different notes, right? Almost right, except that the number 2 hole Draw and the number 3 hole Blow produce the same note. (Mr. Hohner constructed them like that back in the 1830's to make it easier to play German folk music on 'em). So:

Your trusty ten hole harp is made to play 19 different notes.

draw notes on C harmonica

1	2	3	4	5	6	7	8	9	10
D	G	B	D	F	A	B	D	F	A

blow notes on C harmonica

1	2	3	4	5	6	7	8	9	10
C	E	G	C	E	G	C	E	G	C

But by the careful use of bending, you can pull as many as 35 notes from those same ten holes!

draw and draw bend notes on C harmonica

1	2	3	4	5	6	7	8	9	10
D	G	B	D	F	A	B	D	F	A

C#	F#	A#	C#	E	G#	half step bend
	F	A				whole step bend
		G#				step and a half bend

blow and blow bend notes on C harmonica

1	2	3	4	5	6	7	8	9	10
		D#		A#		step and a half up
			F#			whole step up

C	E	G	C	E	G	C	E	G	C

| half step down | | D# | F# | B |
| whole step | | | | A# |

Yes, that's the truth. If you can bend, you can get nearly twice as many notes out of the old tin sandwich as someone who can't bend a harmonica without a vice and monkey wrench. And not only that, but many of these extra 16 notes are the best-sounding, bluesyest notes we'll ever hear. But, to explain why that is I'll have to teach you to read my harmonica notation system, which I call HarpTab™.

For Beginners Who Can't Wait

If any of you beginners just can't wait, you can flip over to **The Pre-Bending Exercise** and **Pre-Bending Licks** section on page 22 and start practicing that *while* you read the rest of the beginner's sections. And if you're in the mood for more "mouth-on" work, spend a few moments working on the **Single Note** section on page 28 — it will really help your bending!

You would probably be wise, on your way to page 22, to glance at all of the **boldface** material, and all of the suggestions that are set off by "bullet" dots like •. But if you've got to blow, you can just go for the Pre-Bends, and come back to the other stuff a little later.

My Notation System: Un-Bent Notes

My notation system is pretty simple to understand:

D = a draw note   **B** = a blow note

The numbers **1 - 10** refer to the numbers 1 - 10 on top of your harmonica. So if I wanted you to play the first four notes of *Oh When The Saints* (number 4 hole blow, number five blow, number 5 draw and number 6 blow), I'd notate them as:

oh	when	the	saints
4	*5*	*5*	*6*
B	*B*	*D*	*B*

Get the idea? If I want you to play two or more notes at one time (that's called a *chord*), I underline

them, like this:
45
D

It's About Time

For songs or licks that don't have words to show
you how long to hold each note, I use a system of
timing dots. Try tapping your foot in a steady beat
while saying:

•   •   •   •

one and two and three and four

Each dot • shows you where the downbeat falls,
that is, exactly when your foot should be hitting
the floor. Each "and" occurs during the upbeat,
when your foot is in mid-air between taps.

Sometimes (especially if it begins on an upbeat) I'll
start a song or lick with four or three downbeats in
parentheses, just like musicians usually count off
"One, Two, Three, Four!" (or "One, Two, Three!")
right before beginning a song on the fifth or fourth
beat. These "count-off" beats are only tapped out
once, at the beginning of the song (or the first time
you play a repeated lick).

Here's *Oh When The Saints* with timing dots instead
of words. Remember, the notes that are in-between the dots should occur when your foot is in
mid-air.

one two three

(• • •)   •   •••

          4   *5*   *5*   *6*
          B   *B*   *D*   *B*

My Notation System: Bent Notes

I indicate a bent note by attaching a little **b** to the
right side of the **D** or **B** (draw or blow) symbol.
For instance, if I wanted you to play a number 2
hole draw bend note, or a number 10 hole blow
bend note, I could notate them like this:

2   *10*
Db   *Bb*

But it's not quite that simple, because you probably remember that some notes can produce up to three different bends, and we have to be able to tell them apart.

Degrees Of Bending: One Half Step

Please look at the diagram of the bent draw notes of the C harmonica, on page 9. You will notice that I have listed only one bent note for holes number 1, 4, 5, and 6. I've listed two bent notes for hole number 2, and three bent notes for hole number 3.

You can see that the unbent number 1 draw note is a D, and its only bent note is a C# (pronounced "C sharp").

draw and draw bend notes on C harmonica

1	2	3	4	5	6	7	8	9	10
D	G	B	D	F	A	B	D	F	A

1	2	3	4	5	6		
C#	F#	A#	C#	E	G#	half step bend
	F	A				whole step bend
		G#				step and a half bend

Now look at this picture of a piano keyboard, with the letter names of each note. The two notes of the 1 draw, D and C#, are right next to each other on the keyboard. The musical distance between them (or any other two notes that are right next to each other) is called one half step.

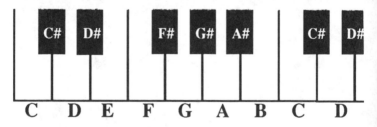

Look carefully at the other draw notes that have only one bent note (4, 5, and 6). You will see that the distance between each unbent and bent note is also one half step. Hole number 4's unbent D to bent C# is the same as number 1, hole number 5 is unbent F to bent E, and hole number 6 is unbent A to bent G#.

We notate bends of one half step with a little b that is higher than the bottom of the D and the B, like:

1	*4*	*5*	*6*
Dᵇ	*Dᵇ*	*Dᵇ*	*Dᵇ*

Degrees Of Bending: One Whole Step

Now look at draw hole number 2, with its unbent note G and bent notes F# and F. The musical distance between G and F# is once again one half step, but the distance between G and F is one whole step. 2 draw is the only draw note with just two bent notes.

We notate bends of one whole step with a little b that is exactly lined up with the bottom of the D and the B, like this number 2 hole draw that is bent all the way:

$$2$$
$$Db$$

Degrees Of Bending: One And A Half Steps

Now look at draw hole number 3, with its unbent note B and its three bent notes A#, A, and G#. The musical distance between B and A# is once again one half step, the distance between B and A is one whole step, and the distance between the unbent B and the most bent note G# is called one and a half steps. 3 draw is the only draw note with three bent notes. It is the trickiest of the draw notes to bend, because you must learn to get all four notes (B, A#, A, and G#) clearly out of that single draw hole. With a bit of practice, you will be able to hit each note as cleanly and clearly as though you were hitting a key on a piano keyboard!

We notate bends of one and a half steps with a little b that is lined up below the bottom of the D and the B, like this number 3 hole draw that is bent all the way to get an G# note:

$$3$$
$$D_b$$

And, to help you get used to the notation used for the different degrees of bending, here are all of the notes that can be played using the number 3 hole draw:

$$3 \quad 3 \quad 3 \quad 3$$
$$D \quad D^b \quad D_b \quad D_b$$

The Blues Scale

Whenever we play a particular type of music, whether it is classical music or the blues, we use what is called a *scale*. A scale is a group of notes that are traditionally used to play a certain type of music. The most well-known scale is the familiar **Major Scale**, or Do Re Mi. It is used for playing most classical and folk music. But the scale that we are mainly interested in is the **Blues Scale**, which is almost always used when playing blues or rock music. In fact, if you study the notes used in your favorite blues and rock songs, you will find that most of them are chosen from the notes of the Blues Scale!

This is a pretty skimpy explanation of a fascinating and important subject, so if you would like to learn more about scales, I suggest that you check out my *Instant Blues Harmonica* book and tape (see page 64) for more complete information.

On the harmonica, the blues scale is most often played in what is called "Cross Position" or "Second Position" (and if you want to know more about positions please see page 64). The easiest way to play a **Cross Blues Scale** requires a one half step bend on the 3 draw, and a one half step bend on the 4 draw:

2	3	4	4	4	5	6
D	*D^b*	*B*	*D^b*	*D*	*D*	*B*

The notes of this scale, which I do not expect you to be able to play yet, are the notes that blues, rock and jazz players will be using the most. Of course, you could play a Blues Scale without bending at all, but it wouldn't sound very bluesy. And that's why you're learning to bend! So don't feel discouraged that you can't play the Blues Scale yet, or the Blues licks and riffs that follow. You are learning how bending is used, and that will help you to use bending as soon as you learn the physical techniques...

About Blues Licks and Riffs

Licks and Riffs are two names for the same thing: short combinations of notes that sound good together. Not all licks or riffs require bending, but most of the best sounding ones do. I'd like to describe a few of my favorite riffs, and their bends, just to give you an idea of the ways in which bends can be used. I'll teach you how to actually play these *after* you've practiced a bit of bending. By the way: Very often, a single great lick is used in dozens or even hundreds of songs, though some of the songs may be better known than others.

A Great and Oft-Used Lick

For instance, take this one, sometimes known as the "I'm A Man" style lick (after one famous song that uses it), which requires a one half step bend on the third note. Please notice that this is not a two beat lick, even though the four notes take two beats (two timing dots) long to play. This is a four beat lick, because each time you play it, you must include the two beats of silence at the end. And remember, you will only play the count-off the first time you play the lick, *not* in between each lick.

one two three

(• • •)   •   •   • •
                                        (two silent beats)

   2   4   3   2

   D   *B*   *D^b*   *D*

If you like, you can play it without the bend on the 3 draw. But it has a very "wimpy" sound without that bend. And if you want to get really fancy, and make the lick sound even more biting, you can use a double bend (which I'll describe in detail, later) on the 3 and 4 draw notes. I notate double bends by putting a line under the two notes that should be bent together, like this:

one two three

(• • •)   •   • • •

   2   4   <u>34</u>   2

   D   *B*   *D^b*   *D*

Double bends take lots of both air and tongue strength, but they are a great technique!

Another Great Lick

This eight beat lick, sometimes called the "Spoon-ful" style lick, also requires a one half step bend on the 3 draw, and ends with one beat of silence.

| • | • | • | • | • • | • | • |

| 3 | 2 | 3 | 2 | 3 | 2 |
| D^b | D | D^b | D | D^b | D |

Like the "I'm A Man" style lick, you can play it without the bends, but it just doesn't sound as hot. And if you want it to sound even hotter, replace each 3 draw half step bend with a double <u>34</u> bend, and throw in an extra 3 draw whole step bend on the last "spooooon", like this (notice the different placement of the bend symbol **b** on the last two bends):

| • | • | • | • | • | • | • | • |

| <u>34</u> | 2 | <u>34</u> | 2 | <u>34</u> | 3 | 2 |
| D^b | D | D^b | D | D^b | D_b | D |

I hope that these examples have given you some idea of why bending is essential to bluesy sound-ing licks and riffs, and maybe even some idea of how advanced bending techniques can be used to make good licks sound even better!

Now I'd like to help you to explore your mouth and tongue, because understanding what goes on in there will help you bend quicker, cleaner, and better!

Exploring Your Mouth

Most of the work of bending is done by the tongue. I've learned a lot about tongues in my twenty years of harmonica playing, and one of the first things that I learned was that I had never learned much about my tongue.

So in the interests of reducing our lingual igno-rance, let's take a quick trip through our mouths, using our tongue as a sort of of exploratory tool. We'll see if we can learn to identify the parts of the mouth by how they feel, even if they lurk far from the light of day. This will help us agree on the terms that I'll use to describe tongue position during bending.

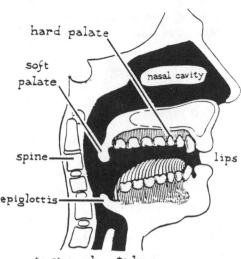

* Begin by touching the back side of your lower front teeth with the tip of your tongue. That's it, do it right now. Un-huhhh.

* Locate the place at the bottom of your lower front teeth where they meet the gums.

* Keep moving the tip of your tongue down, into the "trough" at the very front of the bottom of your mouth.

* Continue even further down and back in your mouth. Can you feel the membrane that connects your tongue to the bottom of your mouth?

* Now touch the back side of your upper front teeth with the tip of your tongue.

* Reach up a fraction of an inch, and feel the place where your upper front teeth meet the gums.

* Continue back along the roof of your mouth for another fraction of an inch, until you feel the hard ridges.

* Keep going back until the roof of your mouth becomes hard and smooth. This is your hard palate. What does it feel like there? The bottom of a boat, maybe?

* Continue even further back until the roof of your mouth becomes slightly softer. This is the soft palate. Touching it with your tongue may tickle, or even trigger your gag reflex.

* Place the tip of your tongue on the upper surface of your left rearmost bottom molar. Touch the upper surface of each tooth until you reach your right rearmost bottom molar. Go back from right to left along your toothtops, and count each tooth

with your tongue. Does the top of each tooth feel different? Some are flat, others sharp. others in-between...

• Do the same thing with the bottom surfaces of your upper molars, from left to right, then back again from right to left.

• Now use your tongue tip to identify the right side of the bottom surface of your left-hand upper molars (that's the side closest to your tongue). Read that over again if you need to. Do it again.

• Use your tongue tip to identify the left side of the bottom surface of your right-hand upper molars (that's also the side closest to your tongue). Do it again.

• Now go back and see if you can do all of these exercises while you hold your lips in the position that you would use when trying to blow out the candles on your birthday cake.

Your Amazing Tongue

Take some time, and play with your tongue. It's a fascinating muscle, rather more like the trunk of an elephant than like your arm or your leg, since it is composed of ten different muscles. Six are internal muscles, connected only to each other; and four are external muscles, that anchor the tongue to various parts of the mouth. These muscles allow us to move the tip and sides and middle of the tongue independently.

Tongue Exercises

Yes, the idea of exercises for the tongue sounds like a joke, but it's not. A well-trained tongue is your best friend, when it comes to bending!

There are two main types of tongue bending exercises, one type to learn tongue position, and the other for strength. For position, work espe-cially with these three tongue exercises: the "Flat Molar Tongue", the "Sliding Drawer", and the "Itchy Palate Humped Tongue".

• **The Flat Molar Tongue:** First, do the last two exercises of the "Exploring Your Mouth" section once more. Now flatten your tongue (as though you were saying the "yyy" part of the syllable "oyyy") so that you can feel the right side of the bottom surface of your left-hand upper molars with the upper rear left side of your tongue, and so you can feel the left side of the bottom surface of your right-hand upper molars with the upper rear right side of your tongue. Confused? Look at the silly guy in the cartoon. Do the two previous exercises a few more times. It's important, because your tongue will often be in a position similar to this when you bend.

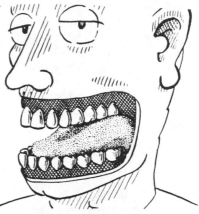

• **The Sliding Drawer ("Oy-You")**: Put your tongue into flat molar position, as in the cartoon. Now, keeping your tongue *firmly pushed up* against your molars, slide your entire tongue towards the back of your mouth, as though your tongue were a drawer that was suspended from the drawer runners that are your upper molars. If you have wisdom teeth, you will feel them with the sides of your tongue as it moves backwards. If not, you will feel the gums behind your molars. Move your tongue back (keeping it *pushed up*, remember) until it becomes uncomfortable (almost as though you were swallowing it). For some people, saying "Oy-You" very slowly helps to form this motion. We'll use lots of "Oy-You" type sounds later on.

• **The Humped-Up Tongue:** The six internal muscles allow our tongues to bend in any direction. These muscles also allow us to create a hump in the middle of our tongue, by raising up just the central muscles.

Imagine this: You're in a fancy restaurant, and all of a sudden the roof of your mouth starts to itch. Let's say that the roof of your mouth is itching too far back for you to scratch the itchy place with the tip of your tongue. And you're way too polite to stick your finger or a fork in there to scratch. So what you might do would be to raise the middle part of your tongue up to create a hump, and to rub that hump against the itchy roof of your mouth.

This "moving middle hump" motion is somewhat similar to the tongue position and movement required for certain bends.

For strength, try these four isometric (without moving) exercises:

• Push your tongue straight up into the roof of your mouth. Hold it there, as firmly as you can, for a count of five.

• With your teeth in a closed position, push your tongue firmly to the left, against your teeth. Hold it there for a count of five.

• Do the same to the right side.

• With your teeth in a closed position, push your tongue firmly against your front upper and lower teeth. Hold it there for a count of five.

Don't push too hard at first, as you don't want to strain your tongue muscles. But as your tongue gets stronger, which may take a week or so, feel free to push more firmly and to hold the tension for more than a count of five. Do some tongue exercises at a boring meeting, or on the bus. Might as well, since no one else can see what you're doing!

Articulation

Using the tongue to break up the airstream on either the inhale or the exhale is called articulation. Please practice some articulations by *whispering* these words. See if you can make the proper tongue motions without making any sound at all. Do it using any comfortable amount of air, and then try it using a lot of air (but still trying to make as little sound as possible).

Nonsensical though they may seem, all will be used in bending effects (I'm really *not* just making cruel fun at your expense with these tongue contortions). For now, just observe the movement and placement of your tongue while you articulate. The "oy"s are especially important, so really exaggerate the mouth movements and observe them closely.

kah   kaka   dada   doo   dahdoo   you

you-you-you   oy   oy-oy-oy   oy-you

If you like, practice some timed combinations of these articulations. Here are a few that form the rhythm patterns for some popular bent riffs. Tap your feet along with the timing dots — it will help later on!

• • • •   • • •   •

you you you   **oy oy oy**

• • • • •   • • •

dada dada dada dada dahdoo dah dah

• • • • • •   • •

dada doo dada doo dada doo dah

In-Articulation

Everybody can articulate while exhaling — it's the same as talking. Articulating on the in-breath takes a bit more practice, so you'd better do some right now! Here's how:

• Start with your lungs pretty empty.

• Keep your nose completely closed. Not sure how to do that? Just read the following section.

• Try to *whisper* the words as you inhale. The first few times will feel awkward, but it really isn't too hard with just a couple of minutes of practice.

Harp players must be able to articulate on both the in and out breath!

Once these articulations have begun to feel comfortable, begin doing them with your mouth in candle-blowing-out position (just a single, small hole). Now practice them through your harmonica, in and out.

The Closed Nose

Now I'd like to teach you to recognize and even use a muscle group that you probably don't know you have. Stand in front of a mirror, and open wide. If you really want to see what's going on in there, shine a flashlight at the very back of your throat while you do this.

Breathe normally, with your tongue lying relaxed in your mouth. Notice that if you want to breathe through your nose only, you must raise the back of your tongue to block the air from passing through your throat.

Now here's the exciting part. Breathe normally again, without making any attempt to avoid breathing through your nose. Suddenly change to breathing through your mouth only, as though you were preparing to cough or blow out. You will see your soft palate (with its dangling "uvula") rise and move (arrow) to the rear of your mouth to block off your nasal cavity, and thus prevent passage of air through your nose. Saying "gung" will have a similar, if less pronounced, effect.

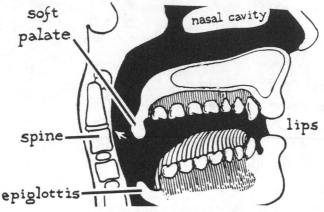

You **must** always keep your nose closed off when bending. You may open your nose to help you take a quick breath *in between* bent or unbent notes. But you **must** keep your soft palate raised (to close the nose) when you bend or try to bend. No one can bend with their nose open!

The Pre-Bending Effect

This technique will allow you to obtain a sound similar to a weak double bend (bend of two holes at a time) right away. It only works on the number 4 and 5 draw notes, and you can do it on any key harmonica. Since it requires the "Oy-Oy-Oy" articulation described in the last section, I some-times call it the "Oy-Oy-Oy" effect. To do it:

• Start with your lungs pretty empty.

• Keep your nose completely closed.

• Place your lips over the number 4 and 5 holes.

• Say "Oy-Oy-Oy" while you inhale. It may be easier to think of it as "Oy-Yoy-Yoy" if you prefer. Start with your mouth very open and your tongue loose in the bottom of your mouth for each "O" part, and end up in the "flat molar" tongue posi-tion (re-read page 18 if you need to) for each "y" part. This means really dropping your jaw to exaggerate the difference between the "O" part and the "y" part (or the "aw" part and the "yee" or "ee" part, as some students prefer to call them).

Some people like to gently bite the sides of their tongues between upper and lower molars during the "y" part, and fling their jaws wide for the "o" part. Others like to think of the articulation as a "yoi", with, of course, the tongue flat for the "y" sound and the mouth opened rapidly for the "oi". Whatever you do, try to emphasize the flatness of tongue and blocked-ness of mouth for the one part, and the openness inside the mouth for the other.

You will hear the sound quality of the two notes change as you articulate each syllable. When you eventually learn to do "real" double bends, you will be able to get a far more dramatic sound change between the "bent" part ("y") and the unbent note. But the "Oy" partial bend is better than nothing, for now, and a good preparation for "real" bending!

Pre-Bending Licks

This technique can actually be quite effective, and it is often used by musicians who like to play harp on their songs but who are not primarily harp players. Perhaps the two best known of these are Bob Dylan and John Lennon.

Bob Dylan Style Pre-Bending Lick

Dylan uses licks similar to this in many of his songs. His *114th Subterranean Dream* is a favorite of mine, with a riff of this type in-between nearly every verse. I'll start you off with the timing of the "Oy" part alone, presented as a four beat lick (three beats of "oy", and one silent beat). This isn't really much of a lick, but practicing it will help you with the actual eight and sixteen beat Dylan style licks.

oy	*oy*	*oy*	
●	●	●	●
45	**45**	**45**	
D	*D*	*D*	

After you feel comfortable with that, incorporate it into an eight beat lick (with three beats of silence). Play it continuously for a while (begin the first "oy" right after you've tapped out the three beats of silence).

oy	oy	oy			
•	•	•	•	•	• • •
<u>45</u>	<u>45</u>	<u>45</u>	<u>45</u>	3	
D	D	D	B	D	

It will actually sound more exciting if, instead of giving the third "oy" and the blow note a full beat each, you cut the third "oy" off short ("oy!") and begin the blow note while your foot is in the air between the third and fourth beat. Then hold the blow note for one more beat before going on to the 3 draw and the three beats of silence. In other words, the third "oy!" has only one half of a beat, and the 45 blow has one and a half beats, like this:

oy	oy	oy!			
•	•	•	•	•	• • •
<u>45</u>	<u>45</u>	<u>45</u>	4 5	3	
D	D	D	B	D	

Dylan often leaves the last three beats silent, as above, but sometimes he fills them in with notes like this:

oy	oy	oy!		
•	•	•	•	•
<u>45</u>	<u>45</u>	<u>45</u>	4 5	3
D	D	D	B	D

•		•	•
2	2	3	4
D	D	D	B

And for a really nice sounding lick, play the first half of the eight beat lick twice, then play the entire eight beat lick once to form a sixteen beat lick.

oy	oy	oy!	
•	•	•	•
<u>45</u>	<u>45</u>	<u>45</u>	4 5
D	D	D	B

oy	oy	oy!		
•	•	•		•
<u>45</u>	<u>45</u>	<u>45</u>	4	5
D	*D*	*D*	*B*	

oy	oy	oy!			
•	•	•	•	•	• • •
<u>45</u>	<u>45</u>	<u>45</u>	4 5		3
D	*D*	*D*	*B*		*D*

A Dylan Style Blues Verse

Blues songs are often divided into verses, and each verse is usually 48 beats long. This type of blues is called **The Twelve Bar Blues Structure**, and I explain it in great detail in my book *Instant Blues Harmonica*, if you are not already familiar with this most important of American art forms.

To play a Twelve Bar Blues , Dylan style, do the following. One "bar" of blues is four beats long, so a twelve bar blues is four times twelve, or 48 beats long. To get those 48 beats:

• Play any of the eight beat licks four times (8 times 4 = 32). I usually play one eight beat lick with the extra 22 3 4 notes, then one eight beat with the three silent beats, then one with the 22 3 4 again, then one with the silent beats.

• Then finish with the sixteen beat lick (32 + 16 = 48 beats or 12 bars).

A Dylan Style Blues "Turnaround"

A "turnaround" is a part of a blues verse that lets the listener know that the verse is ending, and that a new one is about to begin. A turnaround usually occupies the last few beats of the Twelve Bar Blues Structure. For a really easy turnaround that sounds fine, insert a few beats of 1 Draw into the silent beats of the sixteen beat lick, like this, and use this new turnaround version of the sixteen beat lick at the end of each verse.

oy   oy   oy!

●   ●   ●   ●

<u>45</u>   <u>45</u>   <u>45</u>   4   5

D   D   D   B

oy   oy   oy!

●   ●   ●   ●

<u>45</u>   <u>45</u>   <u>45</u>   4   5

D   D   D   B

oy   oy   oy!

●   ●   ●   ●   ●   ●   ●

<u>45</u> <u>45</u> <u>45</u>   4   5   3   1   1

D   D   D   B   D   D   D

John Lennon Style Riff

This lick is similar to one of my favorite Beatle harmonica licks, the one that John used in *I Should Have Known Better*. It is sixteen beats long, and uses a double "oy" rather than the triple "oy" of the Dylan style lick.

oy   oy

●   ●   ●   ●

<u>45</u> <u>45</u>   <u>56</u>   <u>56</u>   <u>56</u>

D   D   B   D   B

oy   oy

●   ●   ●   ●

<u>45</u> <u>45</u>   <u>56</u>   <u>56</u>   <u>56</u>

D   D   B   D   B

oy   oy

●   ●   ●   ●   ●   ● ● ●

<u>45</u> <u>45</u>   <u>45</u>   <u>45</u>   <u>45</u>   <u>34</u>

D   D   B   D   B   D

Sometimes I like to play this one as an eight beat lick, by taking the first four beats and adding an extra beat of 45 draw and three beats of silence.

oy	*oy*				
●	●	●	●	●	●●●
<u>45</u>	<u>45</u>	<u>56</u>	<u>56</u>	<u>56</u>	<u>45</u>
D	*D*	*B*	*D*	*B*	*D*

I then take the new eight beat lick, play it twice, and finish off with the sixteen beat Lennon style lick. It makes for a rocking little 32 beat sequence, if you emphasize those "oy"s!

The Pre-Bending Blues Scale Riff

I'll be straight with you. Trying to play a Blues Scale without bending is like trying to bake chocolate chip cookies without the chocolate chips. But playing a simplified version of the Blues Scale with the "oy" effect won't sound *too* bad, and will prepare you for the real thing!

			oy	*oy*		
●	●	●	●	●	●	● ●
2	3	4	<u>45</u>	<u>45</u>	5	6
D	*D*	*B*	*D*	*D*	*D*	*B*

Try a version going from high to low, also, with a slightly different timing (notice the 3 draw that falls during an upbeat):

		oy	*oy*			
●	●	●	●	●	● ● ●
6	5	<u>45</u>	<u>45</u>	<u>45</u>	3	2 2
B	*D*	*D*	*D*	*B*	*D*	*D D*

If you can play these Blues Scale riffs clearly, and with good crisp single notes where I've notated single notes, then they will actually sound pretty good, for pre-bent licks! And you'll be ready to go for some real bends!

But — and for most new harp players, a big but — if you're not good at single noting yet, it's time to get to work...in the next section.

Getting Single Notes

If you can't get single notes, you probably won't be able to bend. It's as simple as that. Sure, it's possible to bend two notes at once. But it takes a lot of wind and a lot of tongue control, and it is only useful in two places, on the 45 draw and the 34 draw. So if you can't play clear single notes at will, it's time to put some work into it now.

Three Ways To Do It

There are three main ways of getting single notes, but one of them is far and away the best if you want to bend. I'll describe that one, the pucker method, first, then I'll discuss the other two (and why they're not much good for benders).

The Pucker Method

To get a single note using the pucker:

• Make a small round hole with your lips, as though you were whistling, or blowing out a birthday cake, or drinking through a straw.

• This will involve consciously crimping in the corners of your lips, since the natural lip position is wider, good for getting two or three harmonica holes at once (which is called a chord).

natural   small round

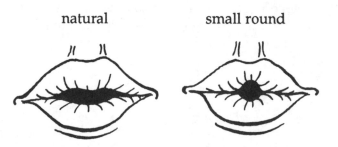

• Your upper lip should be curled slightly up towards your nose, like a dog snarling, rather than down toward your chin like a camel sneering.

• Put your upper lip well over the cover of the harp, and your lower lip well under it. The wet inner part of your lips should be in contact with the harmonica, not the dry outer part. Eat that tin sandwich!

• Begin work with the number 1 or 10 hole. They are the easiest, since there's no chance of a number 0 or 11 sneaking in. Keep your nose closed.

• Even though your lips may feel a bit tense, try to keep your mouth open inside and your throat relaxed.

• **Practice! But don't stop here.** Continue to read this book, and keep playing the licks, songs, and scales from the beginning of the book to at least page 41.

The Tongue Block Method

If you don't know what tongue blocking is, don't even read this section. But if you've been using the tongue blocking techniques to get single notes, then this is a great time to start learning to get single notes by the pucker method, above.

It's really hard to learn bending when using the tongue blocking method, because the side of your tongue is always pushed up against the harp to block three out of the four holes that you are covering with your lips. So your tongue is not free to easily make the movements necessary to bend. If you've already learned to play using the tongue blocking method, it may not seem worth your while to learn the pucker method now. But, I guarantee you, it will be *far* easier to spend a few hours now learning the pucker method, compared to the extra difficulty of learning to bend with the tongue blocking method.

Sorry, but I've been through this with many hundreds of tongue blockers who wanted to learn to bend (some of whom had been tongue blocking for 30 or 40 years), and it's been true for nearly all of them.

The Tongue Curl Method

If you are one of the 50 percent of humanity who is able to curl his or her tongue into a little "u" shape in front, you may have learned to get single notes by putting the "u" curl of your tongue right up against the face of the harmonica. Please read what I told your tongue blocking friends just above, then start workin' on your pucker. Sorry!

The Major Scale

Some of you may poo-poo the Major Scale, thinking it good only for nursery rhymes and simple folk songs. But it will soon provide us with a wonderful exercise for perfecting the pitch (highness and lowness) of our bends, and it is good practice for single noting. Without bending, we can only play a Major Scale in the mid-range of the harmonica. But with it, we can play Major Scales from end to end of the Mississippi Saxophone! Here it is, and be ready for that breathing pattern shift: from B to D on 4, 5, and 6, to D to B on 7. Single note it if you can, if not, stay as single as possible.

do	re	mi	fa	so	la	ti	do
4	4	5	5	6	6	7	7
B	D	B	D	B	D	D	B

A Major Scale Song

Here's my favorite Major Scale song. Practice it now, so that you know how it sounds, and I'll give you an exciting, bent version later on! Since it is pretty easy, I'll use smaller notation.

Oh When The Saints

oh	when	the	saints	go	march	ing	in
•		•••		•		•••	
4	5	5	6	4	5	5	6
B	B	D	B	B	B	D	B

•		•		•	•	•	•••
Oh	when	the	saints	go	march	ing	in
4	5	5	6	5	4	5	4
B	B	D	B	B	B	B	D

•		••		•	•		••
Yes	I	want	to	be	in	that	num	ber
5	4	4	4	5	6	6	6	5
B	D	B	B	B	B	B	B	D

•		•	•	•	•	•••
When	the	saints	go	march	ing	in
5	5	6	5	4	4	4
B	D	B	B	B	D	B

General Instructions

Okay. You now understand what bending is, why it's important, and how generally it's done. You've practiced the pre-bending effect and licks, and can get single notes. It's time to go for it, and start to work on each of the bent notes that can be pulled out of your trusty ten-holer.

Before explaining each specific bend, I'm going to give you a few last general instructions that I've found useful in working with my harp students. I don't expect all of them to be useful for everybody, since everybody's mouth and mind work a little bit differently. But at least a few will help you, so read them all, and think about them, to find the ones that work for you.

I sometimes run into students who listen to my description of tongue position and say "But that's not what's happening inside *my* mouth." Due to the fact that everybody's body is a bit different, this is occasionally true. But much more often, when I ask them to really work at visualizing the inside of their mouth, they say "You know, that *was* pretty much what was happening. I guess it's hard to tell what goes on in there..." It is hard to tell. And maybe your mouth is different. But give these instructions a chance, and they'll give you a chance — to bend!

I will be using the ideas and techniques explained in each of these following sections as I describe how to obtain the different bends. So you may want to return to these sections for help and inspiration as you work on getting each bent note.

In many ways, these general instructions will be more important to you than the specific instructions for each bend. Please use them, over and over, whenever you get stuck!

Also: there is a lot of information in the rest of this book — enough to teach you to bend as well as a top amateur or decent professional harpist, if you master it all. That will take time and practice, so don't get discouraged. It took me nearly a decade to learn to do everything that I tell you about...

Listening To The Slowest Tongue

You're going to have to learn to move your tongue more slowly and more delicately than you ever have — a hundredth of an inch at a time. You'll also need to be observing your tongue closely as you try to bend, staying aware of where it is at every second. That's because you're going to have to learn to locate a place with your tongue, a very, very specific place, and then be able to find it again whenever you want. There's only *one* tongue position that will cause the note to bend like you want it to.

If you have trouble telling where your tongue is, go back to the mouth explorations on page 16, and do them, perhaps with your eyes shut. Focus all of your attention on your tongue. This will increase your awareness of tongue position within your mouth.

You will also have to *listen* very carefully as you work, because you'll probably come across your first real bend by accident. Your tongue will just fall into the right place, and you'll say, "Gee, the note *really* changed that time. Oh boy." Because when you do get a real bend, you'll know it. That note really does sound different. And then by isolating the exact motion that you were making, and trying to recreate it (which may take some time, and be frustrating), you can figure out just where your tongue was when the note bent.

Remember: you are basically using the middle and back of your tongue to tighten up the opening in the back of your throat. This changes the air flow, and causes the bend.

You will also need to use your soft palate (for **The Disgusting Snore Effect**) and possibly even your lips (for **The Harp Tilt Cheat Technique**). But I'll talk about these later on.

The Whee-Oh

Please say the syllable "whee" in a normal voice, and then say "oh" in the lowest voice you can manage. Whee-oh. When you said "whee", your mouth was probably open fairly wide and your lips were also open widely, with your tongue laying relaxed in your mouth. When you dropped down to the "oh", your tongue probably pulled back into your mouth, your jaw dropped and your lips tightened up into a smaller hole.

This is somewhat similar to the motion we're going to make for many bends: moving our tongue back in our mouths and tightening up our lips slightly. It is especially close to the bend motions for draw holes number 1 and 2.

Say "whee-oh" a few more times. You might want to try saying it with your lips in the small candle blowing out hole. This may help you to concentrate on the motion your tongue is making, and is more similar to the actual bending mouth position (since you will usually be single noting).

The Whistling Analogy

If you can whistle, you probably know how to make your whistle sound go from a higher note to a slightly lower one by using a "whee-oh" type repeated tongue motion. Most whistlers change the whistled note by a musical distance of one whole step when they do this. This is the musical distance between 4 draw and 4 blow, or 6 draw and 6 blow.

If you are a whistler, thinking of this may help you to bend, especially on the higher draw notes like 4, 5, and 6. And if you're not a whistler, you're missing out on a great way to do blues/jazz improvisation anywhere — get my book and recording, *How To Whistle Like A Pro*!

The Clutch Analogy

Those of you who know how to drive a car with a clutch may find my clutch analogy useful, especially on the draw notes. Now when you get into a non-automatic transmission car that you've never driven before, this is what you do:

• You keep your right foot off the gas pedal at first, and your left foot presses the clutch pedal all the way to the floor.

• Still with no gas, you slowly, slowly, slowly start letting the clutch up. When the clutch pedal has come up to a certain point (different for each car), you'll feel the car just barely start to tug forward.

• Then you give it some gas while even more slowly and carefully letting your foot up the rest of the way. The car moves forward, smoothly.

If you just fling your foot off that clutch, either you'll take off like a slingshot, burning rubber, or else the car will just stall right out. So you want to feel for that place where the car starts to tug forward, and then when you've found that place, give it more gas while very, very, very slowly bringing your foot up the rest of the way.

Bending is very much like learning to drive a clutch car.

• You pull your tongue back in your mouth until the note just starts to change a little bit, and then you know that you are approaching the correct tongue position.

• At that point you start increasing your air volume of your draw (perhaps also using the Disgusting Snore Effect) while at the same time moving your tongue back even more slowly and carefully. When you reach the exact right spot, the bend just pops out!

Passing Through The Bend

Unfortunately, bending isn't exactly like driving a car with a clutch. It's like driving a car with a *broken* clutch. Your imaginary broken clutch works like this: When the clutch is all the way down, of course the car won't move. Once the clutch is a certain distance partway up, and you give it some gas, the car will ride just fine. But if you let the clutch up the rest of the way, you'll lose your power, and the car will stop moving. So if you didn't want to have it fixed, what you'd have to learn to do is to drive down the road with your foot in kind of an uncomfortable position, just holding the clutch half in and half out.

And that's exactly what you have to do with your tongue when bending. Learn to hold it in that certain position, somewhere not all the way back, not all the way forward. Just the right position so that enough of the air flow is blocked and the note bends down and stays bent down.

When you're learning each bend, you'll go through that "right place" dozens of times, maybe hundreds. You'll hear the sound briefly change (kind of a "wa-ou-wa"), but no bend. That's the sound of your tongue before it hits the right bend position (the unbent sound), then going through the right position (and getting a brief partial bend) and then passing the right position (so that the note returns to the unbent sound). The higher the note you're working with, the less the far back your tongue must be, and the more likely you are to pass right on through the right spot.

You have to learn to move your tongue slower and slower until you can stop with your tongue in just the right position. Not easy, but very satisfying, when you find it!

The Oy-You

Now it's terribly easy to pass right through the correct tongue position so fast, that you don't even hear where the note starts to bend down just a tiny bit. Many of my students find that the "Oy-You" articulation practice helps them to control their tongue better.

Say "oy". As you finish the "oy", you should end up in the flat molar (page 18) position (sides of your tongue pushed up against molars). Now say "you". Your tongue should pull back (the "sliding drawer, page 19), still pressed up against your upper molars. Do it slowly, and feel the upper side parts of your tongue scrape along those molars. Exaggerate it, "ooyy-yoouuu".

See how slowly you can do it, "oooooyyyyy-yoouuuuuu". Take at least ten or fifteen seconds to complete the motion. The "oy-you" position is especially useful on the 2 and 3 draw holes. But some people find it useful on other notes as well.

Note: for most people and most bends, it doesn't seem to matter very much what you do with the tip of your tongue. It is the position of the back and sides of the tongue (where they change the airstream flow) that matter.

At some point in the "oy-you" travel of your tongue, you will find the correct position to get every draw bend on every key harp. When this happens:

- Either the note will become slightly lower in pitch, or

- The note will disappear entirely.

- Either way, you will know that you are in pretty much the right tongue position, and begin to work with your volume changes.

The slower and more carefully you can "oy-you", the better you'll bend.

On Volume

Most of the above hints deal with tongue position, and it is true that tongue position is crucial to bending. But bending isn't just a matter of correct position — **knowing how to use changes in airstream volume can make the difference between getting and not getting a bend.**

As I said in the Clutch Analogy, increasing volume when you reach the right spot will help pull out the bend. So:

- Begin each attempt to get a draw bend with nearly empty lungs.

- Begin each attempt to get a blow bend with nearly full lungs.

- Of course, your nose is closed. Tightly.

- Start playing the note at low volume, while your tongue is moving back. Listen for the faintest change in sound quality.

- If you think you hear the note lower even slightly, continue (more slowly) to move your tongue back, but **double or triple your air volume!**

- As you increase the air volume, you may want to really pour on the power and use the **Disgusting Snore Effect** as well. **It often helps beginners to get a bend, when all else fails.**

The Disgusting Snore Technique

This is just what you'd expect. With your nose closed, inhale and make the sound you'd use to mimic someone snoring (on the inhale part of the snore). This sound is formed by almost closing the back of your throat, and drawing air through. This vibrates the soft palate.

I actually usually call this a **growl**, because it makes any bend sound harsher, or funkier. It's okay to use the growl on all your bends at first, if it helps you to get them, but eventually you'll want to be able to hit any bend with or without it.

Some people (with lots of wind) can actually get some bends just by growling at high volume. But keep working on tongue position, too.

How Do I Know If I'm Bending?

You'll probably know it when you do. The bent note really sounds different, dramatically lower than the unbent note. And it feels different, too. The inside of your mouth will vibrate a little. You can feel the air coming through differently, perhaps hitting your tongue in a way it usually doesn't. Plus, of course, if you've listened to good harp players in person or on recordings, or to my cassette version of this book, you'll know a bend when you hear yourself do it!

The Harp Tilt Cheat Technique

If you are desperate to get a bend, and nothing else seems to be working, you can try this "cheater" technique. Although it doesn't work well enough to be used while playing, it may help you to hear what the bend sounds like. It works mostly on mid-range draw notes 4, 5, and 6, and works better on high key harps than low ones.

• Make sure you're playing a clear single note.

• Tilt the front of the harp (the part without the holes) down, so that your lower lip covers more of the lower plate, and the flesh of your upper lip blocks part of the hole.

• Double or triple your volume, and try a growl. This should pull an entirely different, lower, note from the hole — your bend!

The Bend Visualization Exercise

It's as simple as it sounds. Picture yourself being able to bend. Think about the note bending as you work on it. Think that note down. Since in addition to writing harmonica books, I also write meditation and psychology books, I could go on and on about why this works. I won't. But try it, because for many people it does the trick. Relax, turn the lights low and the volume of your favorite harmonica album or tape up, and work on thinking your bends...

On Practicing

Since bending is hard work at first, don't try to do too much all at once. You're better off doing four or five short sessions each day rather than one long one that will tire your tongue and mouth (and once they're tired, forget about getting good bends). Put in ten minutes at a time on actual bend practice, then take a break: read this book for some inspiration, if you've got nothing else you have to do while waiting for your next practice session!

Does It All Sound Confusing?

I know. There are an awful lot of things to think about in a very few seconds , while you're trying to bend. But if it's any consolation, think back to when you learned to drive (if you do). Even on a car without a clutch, you had to: steer, use the gas pedal, be ready to brake, look in the rear view mirror, keep an eye on the speedometer, and watch where you were going. It seemed like a lot then, but today you can talk, listen to the radio, maybe even play your harmonica while you drive, (although I'm not recommending that, mind you) without straining in the slightest.

Soon bending will be the same. So just keep in mind what you can, re-read to remember the rest, and don't worry too much...just practice.

Different Harps: Which One To Use

You can learn to bend on any standard ten hole harmonica, no matter what the key. As I've said before, each key harp is different. The lowest commonly available harmonica key is the G (although the Hohner Company makes a special order low D, and the Huang Company makes a few low F and F#'s), and the highest commonly available harmonica is the F or F#. But, in general:

• **The lower the harp key, the larger the tongue motion required to bend each note.**

• **The lower the hole on the harp (1 is lower than 2, and so on), the larger the tongue motion also.**

• **A higher note on a lower key harmonica may use a bend position similar to a lower note on a higher key harmonica.**

For your information (and it may actually be useful to those of you who have lots of different key harps), **here are a few examples of bent notes that use similar tongue positions:**

The G harp 6 draw bend = D harp 4 draw bend = F harp 3 draw half step bend. The A harp 6 draw bend = E harp 4 draw bend. The C harp 2 draw whole step bend = E harp 1 draw bend. The B flat harp 4 draw bend = D harp 3 draw whole step bend = F harp 2 draw whole step bend. The C harp 4 draw bend = E harp 3 draw whole step bend = F harp 3 draw step and a half bend.

For people without much lung power, I'd recommend *not* starting out on a very low harp like a G or an A. In fact, if you are really short on air, an F may be your best bet. The number 1 draw bend on an F is probably the easiest bend of all: doesn't take much air, easy to get as a single note, and neither a very small or a very large tongue motion.

However, it is extremely difficult to blow bend the notes on a harmonica higher than C or D. So if blow bending is important to you (love those screaming high notes, J. Geils style!), use the lower keys, like G or A.

C is a nice mid-range harp to start with, but beginners often have trouble getting a clear note from the 2 draw, which tends to partially bend almost by itself. That might seem like a tremendous advantage (a self-bending harp?), but it really is not, for new harpists. The problem is that if they cannot get a clear unbent 2 draw, it becomes hard to hear the difference (when they eventually get a fully bent 2 draw) between their partially bent 2 draw and their fully bent one. But if you are willing to work patiently with the 2 draw at first, C is not a bad choice.

My real recommendation is to start serious bend work with an F (for the easy draw notes, especially the 1 draw), and an A (for the blow notes).

In my cassette version of *Bending The Blues*, I use an A, F, and C harp to demonstrate each bend (except for the blow bends on the F).

Which Bend(s) To Start On

Try 'em all. Some people find one bend the easiest, others find that same one the hardest. A few hints:

• Almost everyone finds the draw bends easier than the blow bends.

• Try *all* of the draws at once, from 1 to 6, rather than trying to get each one before going on to the next. One may be easy, and give you some encouragement!

• You'll get one, then lose it, then find it again.

• The instructions for each bend are followed by licks using that bend, so when you get a bend, try to use it. But it's easier to *get* a bend at first than it is to *use* it...

Advanced Techniques

I've placed advanced techniques that can be used with all of the bends at the end of the individual bend sections. That *does not* mean that you should wait until you can get all the bends before applying advanced techniques to them. Instead, as soon as you are able to get even one bend, go to the advanced techniques and start applying them to your bend.

The Scales

I've also put all of the scales after the bending sections, on pages 62 and 63. But once you've gotten the bends necessary to try to play a scale, go for it! Here are the bends that you'll need to play:

• **The Middle Second Position Blues Scale** (need 3 draw half step and 4 draw)

• **The Low Second Position Blues Scale** (need 2 draw whole step, 3 draw half step, 1 draw)

• **The High Second Position Blues Scale** (need 6 blow)

• **The High First Position Blues Scale** (need 8 blow half step, 9 blow half step, 10 blow whole step)

• **The Low Major Scale** (need 2 draw whole step, 3 draw whole step)

• **The High Major Scale** (need 10 blow half step)

• **Chromatic Scales** (need them all)

The Bends

Here they are, finally. I'll walk you through number 1 draw more thoroughly than most of the others, so turn back to this one if you need a bit of review. Good luck!

1 Draw

No matter what key harp you have, your 1 draw bend note will require the largest tongue movement. It should also be easy to hit as a single note, since there is no 0 hole to worry about. 1 draw has only one bent note, a half step lower than the unbent note.

• Begin with your lungs nearly, but not completely empty (if they are completely empty you may be tempted to rush, and you don't want to do that).

• Get a good single 1 draw, with as little tension as possible in your tongue and throat.

• Then use the "oy-you" "sliding drawer" (pages 18 and 19) to **slowly** slide your tongue back, until you hear a slight change (lowering) of the sound. Listen carefully.

• With a high harp like an F, you may only need to slide your tongue about half an inch.

• With a low harp, like a G, you may need to slide as much as an inch and a half. With a low harp, it may help to drop your lower jaw, to help pull your tongue way back. On an A or G, it may feel as though you are almost swallowing your tongue.

• As soon as you hear the sound change, increase your volume dramatically without changing your tongue position. Try the growl effect (page 36), too.

• If the note suddenly lowers in pitch, congratulations. You've got a bend!

Troubleshooting

There are really only three main mistakes you can make: tongue not back far enough, tongue back too far, or forgetting to apply volume or the growl when you do get to the right place (your nose *is* closed, right?). Experiment!

• So try again, this time sliding your tongue back a tiny bit *further* before increasing your volume and growling.

• If you hear a slight sound change, but seem to end up on the original unbent note (this may sound something like "ah-wah"), you are probably passing *through* the right place. Move your tongue more slowly, and apply the growl and volume a bit earlier.

• Tightening your lips and protruding them a bit more to make a slightly smaller hole may possibly help. Try it a few times.

• Re-read the above, and try it again and again. It's not unusual for someone to take quite a few hours of practice before they get their first bend. But once the first one comes, the others are easier.

If You Can't Seem To Get It

Don't get discouraged. It took *me* more than four months of trial-and-error between the time I first heard about bending, and the time I got my first full bend (a 2 draw on my C harp). Go on and try some of the other bends, and keep coming back to this one. Re-read the instructions, and try, try, again.

Once You Get 1 Draw Bend

You've gotten it once. Hurrah! Now you have to go back and learn exactly where that bending place is. Memorize it! When you can play the unbent note, and then bend it down fairly reliably (if not every time you try), read about the advanced techniques (page 55). Then I'll give you some licks that use these techniques.

1 Draw Bend Licks

There aren't a lot of hot licks that use only the 1 draw bend. Probably the most satisfying thing you can do with your new bend is to practice the advanced articulation bending patterns on page 56. Make up some "doo" and "dah" patterns of your own, too.

Here's a sixteen beat lick based on the Blues Scale that I like. Remember that a note without a dot over it occurs during the upbeat of the downbeat to the left of it, so in the first line, the 1 draw falls on the downbeat and the 1 draw bend on the upbeat.

•   • • • •   • • •

1 1 1 2   1 1 1 2

D D♭ D D   D D♭ D D

•   • • • • • • •

2 2 3 4 1 1 1 2

D D D B D D♭ D D

2 Draw

I remember when I first learned to bend 2 draw, my first bent note. As soon as I could trust myself to bend it at least half the time I tried, I ran out to look for Wild Ed, a neighbor who could play so little blues guitar that he was willing to jam with me. He played a Twelve Bar Blues, and I just played 2 draw and 2 draw bent notes. It sounded great!

Since 2 draw has two possible bends, the half step and the whole step, it is a bit trickier than 1 draw, although the half step bend is rarely used. So:

• Lungs nearly empty, nose shut, and a good single 2 draw, with as little tension as possible in your tongue and throat. Remember that if you are already partially bending 2 draw without meaning to, it will be hard to hear the actual bend. Not sure if you are? The unbent 2 draw should sound the same as 3 blow.

• Then use the "oy-you" until you hear a slight lowering of the sound.

• As your tongue moves *slowly* back, you may hit a point where the sound seems to disappear. That's a great sign that you're in the right place!

• As soon as you hear the sound lower or disappear, increase your volume dramatically without moving your tongue. Try the growl effect (page 36), too. This is even more useful on 2 draw than on 1 draw.

• With a low harp, it may help to drop your lower jaw a little, to help pull your tongue way back.

• If you hit a 2 draw whole step bend, even for a second, you'll really know it! Since it's a whole step bend, it sounds very different from the unbent note, and you'll really feel the vibration, especially if you use a growl.

Troubleshooting

Please re-read the 1 draw troubleshooting section (page 42). The only other specific problem most people have with 2 draw bent is that they have not worked enough on getting a relaxed 2 draw unbent first.

If you aren't sure whether you're getting half or whole step bends, go on to the Step By Half Step section (page 46).

And don't get hung up on any specific bend. Try some others, and keep coming back!

2 Draw Bend Licks

I assume that you've already read the advanced technique section. Practice a smooth slide from 2 draw to 2 draw bent to 1 draw on the four beat lick, then play this classic eight beat turnaround.

Every blues and rock player uses this one!

```
•       •   •   •
2   2   1
D  Db  D
```

```
•   •       •       •       •       •   •   •
2   2   2   2   2   2   2   2   2   1   1
D   D   D   D   D   D   D   D  Db   D   D
```

or for a fancier turnaround try:

```
•       •   •       •   •       •   •   •
2   2   1   2   2   1   2   2   1   1
D  Db   D   D  Db   D   D  Db   D   D
```

Here's a **James Cotton style** one:

```
•   •   •   •   •       •   •   •
2   3   4   4   2   2   1   1
D   D   B   B   D  Db   D   D
```

Try my favorite 2 draw pattern using "dah" and "doo" articulations . Notice that in one place two 2 draws occur during one upbeat. **John Mayall** uses a pattern similar to this in his famous *Room To Move*:

```
•       •       •           •
2   2   2   1   2   2   2   2   1
D   D  Db   D   D   D   D  Db   D
```

```
•       •       •   •
2   2   2   1   2
D   D  Db   D   D
```

If you really have your 2 draw bend "doo" down, try this lick, similar to the classic **Hoochie Coochie Man lick**, which begins on an upbeat. To hear what it should sound like, play it mid-range.

one two three
```
(• • •)     •           •   •   •
        1   2   1   2   2
        D  Db   D  Db   D
```

```
(• • •)     •           •   •   •
        4   5   4   5   6
        D   D   D   D   B
```

3 Draw

3 draw isn't particularly hard to bend. In fact, a fair number of my students over the years have found their first ever bend lurking in that third hole. But it's hard to control. That's because there are three different possible bends in there, each separated by only a tiny motion of your tongue.

For now, simply try to get *any* bend out of 3 draw, using exactly the same instructions that I gave you on page 44 for the 2 draw. The growl and a dramatic increase in air volume when your tongue is *anywhere* near the correct position may very well give you a bend here (which one, who knows!). In the next section, I will discuss the various bends that can be teased out of the 2 and 3 draw holes.

Step By Half Step

As you know, the 2 draw hole has two distinct bends, and the 3 draw hole can provide three, the most of any draw or blow hole. That's the good news. The bad news is that it takes skillful tongue work to hit each one clearly. Of course, you could argue that the distance between the most bent and the unbent notes could (by a superb bender) be broken up into a dozen different notes. But we only count half steps (the distance between notes on the piano) as legitimate bent notes.

The 2 Draw Bends

On the 2 draw, since there are only two bent note positions, you are either : completely unbent, fully bent (the whole step bend), or somewhere in the middle. Once you learn to hit the fully bent place, you can then just allow your tongue to come halfway forward (towards the unbent position) to find the half step bend (which is very rarely used). Here's a convenient way to practice the full bend. Start out by reviewing the Major Scale, played from high to low end.

7	7	6	6	5	5	4	4
B	D	D	B	D	B	D	B

Now play the following Major Scale, in which you jump from one octave note to a lower octave. **Octave notes,** by the way, are notes in which the speed of vibration of the higher note is exactly twice the speed of vibration of the lower note. This magically makes the two notes sound similar, even though one is higher and one lower. If you don't believe me, ask your harmonica: play 1 blow, then 4 blow, then 7 blow, then 10 blow, all octave notes, just as 2 draw, 6 blow, and 9 blow are...

7	7	6	6	5	2	1	1
B	D	D	B	D	B	D	B

When that feels familiar, try this one, which uses the 2 draw whole step bend. Since you know what the Major Scale notes must sound like, it will help you to locate the full bend by listening as you do it. If you learn to get the 2 bend as a "doo" (page 55), you'll be able to play this from low to high also:

7	7	6	2	2	2	1	1
B	D	D	D	D♭	B	D	B

A Note On Nose Closing

All serious benders eventually run into the **nose close blues**. That's when, even though you are trying to keep your nose shut during a tricky set of bends, some air blasts through (with a disgusting sound, if your nose is near the microphone). What happened is that the muscles of your soft palate got tired, and loosened on you. As you practice, these muscles will strengthen, and it will happen less (or at least take longer to happen). It occasionally still happens to me, especially if I have been doing an outdoors unamplified set (which means playing loud) using lots of bends. I just try to avoid bends for a few minutes, to give my soft palate a rest.

The Three Draw Bends

Only one of the three 3 draw bends, the half step, is commonly used in blues or rock music. Another, the whole step bend, is convenient for folk and country and western music, and occasionally used in blues and rock. The third one, the step and a half bend, isn't used much.

The step and a half bend is easiest for most people to find, since you can't bend any further. Bring your tongue back more, and the note pops back to the unbent, because you went through the bentest position. So it's fairly easy to find: just use lots of air, the growl, and slooowly pull your tongue back until the note pops up to unbent. Then, next time, don't pull back *quite* so far.

One way to help locate the 3 draw whole step bend is to play 7 draw and then 6 draw for a while. These notes are the same as 3 draw unbent and 3 draw whole step bent, only one octave higher.

But probably the best way (once you begin to get any bend sounds out of 3 draw) to find the whole step 3 bend is with the octave jump Major Scale, like you did for the 2 bend whole step. Review the Major Scale on page 30, then try these. The next one is for folks that haven't got 2 draw bend. Make your three bend fit the scale!

4	3	3	2	5	5	4	4
B	D	D♭	D	D	B	D	B

The Low Bent Major Scale

If you can do this, even halfway decently, you're getting to be a darn good bender! Try it going up, once you can "doo" the 2 and 3 draw bends. And begin to play songs in the low octave (1 - 4 range) that you used to do in the mid-range (4 - 7 holes). I'll give you the first part of *Oh When The Saints*, and you can work out the rest by yourself (hint: num-*ber* uses 3 draw whole step bent). What other songs can you play down here?

4	3	3	2	2	2	1	1
B	D	D♭	D	D♭	B	D	B

1	1	2	2	2	3	3	4
B	D	B	D♭	D	D♭	D	B

oh	when	the	saints	go	march	ing	in
•		•••		•		•••	
1	2	2	2	1	2	2	2
B	B	D♭	D	B	B	D♭	D

	•		•	•	•	•	•••
Oh	when	the	saints	go	march	ing	in
1	2	2	2	2	1	2	1
B	B	D♭	D	B	B	B	D

Don't Forget Your Scales

As you start getting more bends, don't forget to work on the scales at the end of the book. The chart on page 41 will tell you what bends you need to play each one.

The Important 3 Draw Bend

I'm talking about the half step bend, of course. It's a Blues Scale note, and for that reason the most important 3 draw bend.

Since it is only a partial bend, it doesn't require much of a tongue movement, and that makes it tricky. On a high harp like an F, all it might take is to hump the middle part of the tongue (remember the itchy mouth roof?) up an eighth or a quarter of an inch *towards* (not touching) the roof of your mouth. Others may bend it by just barely starting the "you" part of an "oy-you", with the tongue moving maybe a quarter of an inch.

On lower harps, like the A or G, the tongue may need to move a bit more. But most people will find it easiest to work on the other 3 draw bends first, and then allow the tongue to move forward from the deeper bend position.

Playing the following licks may help you to locate this note. If you don't bend the 3 draw enough when you play them, they will have a cheerful, tra-la-la kind of sound rather than a bluesy sound. And if you bend the 3 draw too far, they will sound just plain wrong. Bent just right, they sound tense and exciting, but very right!

Here's the **I'm A Man style lick, used in so many songs,** that we studied earlier. Listen for this one in TV commercials, and in modern and classic rock songs.

one two three

(• • •)　•　　　•　　　(two silent　beats)
　　　　　　　　　　　　•　•

　2　4　3　2
　D　B　D♭　D

Now try the **Spoonful style lick**. It's a great one for teaching you to "doo" this bend, since the bend is such an important part of the lick. Then, if you're feeling confident about your 3 draw bends, go back to page 16 and play the version with the half *and* the whole step.

•		•	•		•		••	•		•
3		*2*	*3*		*2*		*3*	*2*		•
Dᵇ		*D*	*Dᵇ*		*D*		*Dᵇ*	*D*		

And here's a great sounding **First Position Hoochie Coochie Style Lick** (if you can "doo" your three bend) that you'll use with your blow bends later on. It's similar to the lick used in Sonny Boy Williamson II's "Don't Start Me To Talkin'".

one two three

(• • •)	•		•	•	•
	2	*3*	*2*	*3*	*4* (silent beats)
	D	*Dᵇ*	*D*	*Dᵇ*	*B*

Of course, as soon as you learn to hit your **double bends**, you can go back and play the "Man" and "Spoonful" style licks with them, as I described on pages 15 and 16.

The Bend Stations of 3 Draw

As you learn to get each of the 3 draw bends, begin practicing like this: start unbent (and very empty), then go to the lowest, step and a half bend. Let your tongue come slowly back up to the unbent position. But instead of coming up in one smooth slide, think of your tongue as a train, stopping at each of four stations: the most bent, the whole step bent, the half step bent, and the unbent. Go quickly from one to the other, stopping to rest for a second at each "station". Soon, it will feel as though your tongue is just "clicking" into position, easy and natural.

After you've learned to do this, do it in the other direction, from unbent to most bent. It's even harder this way — if you can do this, you're bending like a pro!

Double Bends

There are really only two places where double bending works, on 3 and 4 draw and on 4 and 5 draw. But it is such a powerful and bluesy technique that it's a must have for any serious harpist.

You've already got a head start on bending 4 and 5 draw, with the pre-bending effect. The only difference between pre-bending and double bending is that instead of using the "oy-oy-oy", you'll use an "oy-you" type of tongue motion, the same as you've used for all your other bends.

Basically, all you need for the 45 draw bend is **volume**. Position is easy, since neither of these notes have more than one possible bend. Slide into the "you", and listen for the spot where the sound of the unbent 45 draw lowers a bit. This, of course, is somewhere around the "oy" spot you've used in the pre-bending effect. But instead of launching into another "oy", hold your position, increase your volume, try a growl, and your double note will hop down into a bend. It makes a wonderful train whistle! If you have trouble here, work on the 4 draw and 5 draw bends, since their tongue position will be almost the same as needed here.

By the way, double bends are easier, at first, on C harps and higher (less volume needed).

The 34 bend also takes a lot of volume. The majority of my students find it simplest to work on the 34 bend after they have learned to get the 3 draw half step bend, since this double bend is virtually always used to substitute for the 3 draw half step bend. In fact, basically, this double bend is best learned by getting a 3 draw half step bend, then opening the right side of your mouth to let some 4 draw in, without changing your tongue position but while doubling your volume. The growl works great here, too, and will help pull the bend through.

4 Draw

Getting a 4 draw bend is in many ways like getting a 1 draw bend. Both have only one bent note, a half step lower than the unbent note. The same cautions apply:

• Lungs fairly empty, so that you have lots of air to draw on.

• Nose firmly closed, get a good single note, and use the "oy-you" to slide your tongue back.

But the 4 draw bend will take a much smaller tongue movement than the 1 draw, especially on high harps, so it will be easier to miss the right spot by going through it, as described on page 34. It may also feel as though the "action" is taking place further forward than with the 1, so the "itchy mouth hump tongue" analogy may be worth thinking about.

On these higher notes, it often feels to me as though my tongue is like a hooded cobra: powerful, tense, spread out and reared up as though to strike!

A New Hump Tongue Method

As with most other bends, what the tip of your tongue is doing won't make much difference. On high harps, you may even want to brace the tip of your tongue against your lower front teeth, and try to simply create a hump in the middle of your tongue that gets in the way of the air flow. This is the hump that you might raise to scratch the roof of your mouth if it itched about an inch back from your teeth, and for some reason you didn't want to use the tip of your tongue to scratch with.

This hump can be raised or lowered by raising and lowering your lower jaw. For an F harp, this humped area might be about an inch back from the tip of your tongue. For lower keys, like D or E, it might be a bit more.

As usual, listen carefully for a sound change, because when you hear it you'll know that you're close to the correct spot, then increase your air, and try a growl. If you aren't getting anywhere with it for a while, and feel frustrated, try the Harp Tilt Cheat Method (page 37).

4 Draw Riffs

Here are a few of my easiest favorites:

•		•	•		•	•		•	•	•
4	4	3	4	4	3	4	4	3	2	
D	D♭	D	D	D♭	D	D	D♭	D	D	

•	•	•	•	•	•	•	•	•	•	••
4	4	5	6	5	4	4	4	3	2	
D	D♭	D	B	D	D	D♭	B	D	D	

•		•		•		•	•		•	••
4	4	4	4	3	2		4	4	3	2
D	D♭	B	D	D	D		D	D♭	D	D

Don't forget to practice the "doo" and "dah" patterns in the advanced techniques section, and then you'll be able to hit your 4 draw bend already bent, and play these neat riffs, the first a **Sonny Boy Williamson # 1** style, the second more **Sonny Terry** style:

●   ●   ●   ●   ●   ●   ●   ●   ● ●●●

4	4	5	4	4	5	4	4	3	2
D^bD	D	D^b	D	D	D^b	B	D	D	

●   ●   ●   ●

4	4	3	4	3	2	3	2
D^bB	D	B	D	D	D	D	

5 Draw

There isn't much to say about 5 draw. Like 1, 4, and 6 draw, it has only one bend. But in this case, it's barely even a full half step. If you read what I wrote about 4 draw, and apply it all to 5 draw, you probably won't have much trouble. The bend position will be a little less far back than that of 4 draw, otherwise it's pretty similar. The main problem people have with 5 draw is expecting too much out of it — it just doesn't bend that far.

5 draw bend has a bit of a dreamy sound. Most of my favorite 5 bend licks are for third position harmonica, but that's another book. So here are a few of the second position 5 bend licks that I use. Slide down to the 2 in the first one, which has a one two three countoff. The second is from an old J. Geils riff, and uses a repeated "dwah" bend (see page 56) that's almost like an "oy":

(● ● ●)   ●   ●   ●   ●   ●   ●   ●   ●

5	5	4	5	5	2
D	D^b	D	D	D	D

dwah dwah dwah   dwah
● ●   ●   ●   ●   ●   ●   ●

5	5	5	5	5	4	6	6
D	D	D	D	B	D	B	B

dwah dwah dwah   dwah
● ●   ●   ●   ●   ●   ●   ●

5	5	5	5	5	4	2
D	D	D	D	B	D	D

6 Draw

As you probably expect, 6 draw bend requires a very small tongue motion. On a high harp, the slightest waver of the middle of your tongue will bend 6 draw, and it's ridiculously easy to pass through the bent spot. I recommend using the tongue braced on teeth approach to 6 draw (page 52), just humping the middle of the tongue a little, maybe 1/2 or 3/4 of an inch back from the tip for an F, further back for a low harp.

6 draw bend has only the one bent position, and it is more commonly used in jazzier styles, or for playing in minor keys. It does fit in well during the Dominant (or V) chord of a Twelve Bar Blues, so I'll give you two four beat licks to use there, then an eight beat lick similar to that used by **Sugar Blue** in the **Rolling Stones** song **Miss You**:

•	•		•		•
6	6	5	6	5	4
D	D♭	D	D♭	D	D

•		•		•		•
6	6	7	6	5	4
D♭	D	B	D	D	D

•	•	•	•	•	•	•	•
6	6	8	7	6	6	6	
D♭	D	D	B	D	B	D	

The Unbendable 7

There really isn't much that can be done with 7, draw or blow. Sure, you can bend it down a little, but the sound quality isn't much good, the note produced won't be very useful from a blues/rock point of view, and it's bad for the reed. So I recommend leaving 7 alone (on the ten holer, on the chromatic it's another story).

Advanced Techniques

Don't let the title fool you. Yes, these are advanced techniques, but that doesn't mean that you have to have all your basic bends down pat to use them. If you can pull even one uncertain bend out of one hole part of the time, you're ready to read this section, and start to use it!

Doos, Dahs, and Dah-Oohs

As you doubtless remember, articulation means breaking up the airstream with our mouths. You've already (I hope, if not, see page 20) practiced articulating on unbent notes. Now it's time to articulate some bends.

When you take and unbent note and bend it down, you might call that process an "ah-ooh", with "ah" representing the unbent note and "ooh" the bend. If you began the unbent note more sharply, with the articulation "dah", you would call the whole thing a **"dah-ooh"**. If so far you have been beginning your bends by simply drawing on the unbent note (rather than starting it more sharply with a "dah"), practice using a "dah" to get the unbent note that you plan to bend. "Dah-ooh".

Doo-ing A Bend

Now it's time to learn to articulate a note *while* it's bent. Although it's not easy, the closest to an easy way to do it is like this:

• Practice some rapid "doo" articulations on unbent notes, in and out, using the tip of your tongue just behind your upper front teeth.

• Bend your best note, and once you've got it bent, keep it bent. Practice holding it down for as long as possible — it'll get easier fast.

• Bend and hold a note bent, and stop breathing for a second, without changing your mouth or tongue, then start again. The bent note will stop and start, also.

• When you can do that, try articulating a "doo" type of sound to start the bend again after you've stopped breathing for a second.

• See how many "doo"s you can do on one breath's worth of a bend.

I call the above exercise the "dah-ooh-doo-doo-doo". Once you can bend a note down, and "doo" it, it's time to try to *start* a note bent, without bending it down from unbent position. Really watch your tongue as you practice the "dah-ooh-doo-doo-doo", and try to memorize the "doo" tongue position. Then just work on "doo"ing without the "dah-ooh". If you can bend more than one note, try it on all of them.

What To Do With Doos

Once you can get a clear "doo" some of the time, here are some things to try:

• Make some "dah doo" patterns, using any articulated unbent note and its bent note. Here are two of my favorites. They can be used with any notes. The first is similar to **John Mayall's Room To Move** pattern (try it on 2 draw and 2 draw bend), and the second to the rhythm of the song **Tequila**.

```
 •        •    •        •    •        •           •  •
dah dah doo  dah dah doo  dah dah  doo  dah
 •        •    •        •    •        •
doo doo dah  dah doo doo dah  dah doo doo
 •    •    •
dah dah doo
```

• Try some **"doo-wah"s**. In a "doo- wah", you begin a note bent ("doo") and then relax your tongue up to the unbent position ("wah"). An exciting special effect is to "doo" a single note, then open up to *two* holes for the "wah". I most often do this on 3 draw bend half step to 34 draw, or 4 draw bend to 45 draw. It's a great **Country and Western** effect, as in:

•	•	•	•	•	•	•	• • • •
1	*2*	*2*	*3*	*3*	*2*	*3*	*34*
D	*B*	*D*	*D*	*Db*	*D*	*Db*	*D*

A very quick "doo-wah", called a **"dwah"**, is a note that starts bent (with a "doo") but instantly re-leases into the unbent "wah". It's something like an "oy", except for starting with an articulation, and being completely bent at the start. Try some **"Dwah-dahs"** too, in which you add an unbent "dah" after a "dwah". Makes a great rock turn-around:

dah	dwah	dah	dwah	dah	dwah	dah	dah	ooh	dah	dah
•	•		•		•		•		•	•	•
2	*2*	*2*	*2*	*2*	*2*	*2*	*2*	*2*	*1*	*1*
D	*D*	*D*	*D*	*D*	*D*	*D*	*D*	*Db*	*D*	*D*

• Do the reverse too. Begin on a double note like 45 draw, and squeeze it down to a single 4 draw bend. Add a few notes, and you've got a great blues or rock lick:

•	• •		•	• • •		• • •	• •	
<u>45</u>	4	3	2	6		5		
D	D♭	D	D	B		D		

• Try a **"doo wah-ooh"** by hitting a note bent, relaxing up to the unbent note (or two notes), then bending it back down. This makes for a wonderful train whistle.

• Use the **Bent Warble**. In the warble, you rapidly alternate between two neighboring notes, like 4 and 5 draw, with your lips in single note position (a bit of saliva goes a long way, here). Simply move your tongue to the right bend position for the lower note (4 draw bend, in this case), and the entire warble will bend down. Then relax it back up to the unbent warble. J. Geils harpist **Magic Dick** does this throughout most of the third verse of his superb harp song **Whammer Jammer**.

• Use bends with your **hand wah wah**. Do some wahs during a long held bend, or wah wah while you go from unbent to bent, or vice versa. If you are a good hand wah wah-er, learn to do the articulation rhythm patterns above. Then, instead of using your tongue to articulate, use your hand wah wah to break up the notes into the rhythm, with two or three wahs per beat.

• **Slide and Bend, or Bend and Slide.** Simply slide up to a note, then bend it, or slide down to a note and bend it. Or play an unbent note, bend it down, then slide down from the bent note. You can even bend while you slide in the 1 - 6 draw range, although it seems hard to keep bent for more than a few notes, since your tongue position must change as you pass each hole. The 3-2-1 draw bend slide is easiest, for me, and makes an exciting ending for a Twelve Bar.

• Another hard technique involves going rapidly between the full sounding "Octave Block" effect and a deep, growling bent note. It takes a radical and instant change in tongue position, but it's well worth the practice, as this fabulously depressing Charlie Musselwhite style (third position) proves:

• • •		• • • •	•		•		•		•		•		•		• • • • • •		
<u>14</u>		<u>14</u>	3		3		2		2		2		1		1	
D		B	D♭		B		D♭		D		D♭		D		D	

Blow Bending

I'd been playing harp seriously for more than five years before I learned to bend my blow notes. I knew that there were players out there doing these incredibly high, powerful licks, but I figured that they were using some special kind of harp...or something. Once I discovered that high end, I could barely do anything else for weeks (my friends hated me)!

Blow bending is the graduate school of bending, so don't you beginners be in a big hurry to master it. But there's certainly no harm in knowing about it, and experimenting. Blow bends are mostly used in two rather different ways.

• In First Position (harp in same key as the music), you can play almost any song that you can play in the low or middle part of the harp, using lots of blow bends. **Stevie Wonder's** *Boogie On Reggae Woman* is a good example of this. Sometimes blues players (**James Cotton** and **Junior Wells** come to mind here) alternate low end first position draw bend licks with high blow bends, as in the instructions I'll give you below.

• In Second Position, blow bends are used more as punctuation, or to get some high end Blues Scale notes, as in my High End Blues Scale. 9 blow and 9 blow bend will be your most used Second Position blow notes. Sometimes, during the Subdominant or IV chord, a player will use all blow bends (**Magic Dick** likes to do this).

I notate blow bends exactly as I do draw bends. And since the same tongue motion is involved in virtually all of the high blow bends, I'll provide you with generalized instructions rather than dealing with each note separately.

General Instructions

Most of the blow bends involve the highest notes on the lower key harps. It's very difficult to blow bend any note lower than an 8 blow (although it can be done, as discussed below). And it's hard (and shrill, and bad for the reeds) to blow bend the best notes (8 - 10) on a harp higher in key than a D, or even a C. So if you want to learn to blow bend, try to use a G or an A.

I like to describe the tongue motion used in blow bending as an "ah-hiss". To blow bend:

• Get a good single note. 10 is easier to single note, but 8 is usually easier to bend. So if you're good at single noting, use 8. Otherwise, practice — because good single noting is even more essential for blow bending than draw bending.

• Start with your lungs pretty full, nose closed, and mouth open wide and relaxed inside.

•The tip of your tongue should be touching your lower front teeth. Gently play the note: "ah".

• Then brace the tip of your tongue against your lower front teeth, and hump or roll up the middle of your tongue close to the front. Exhale for the "hiss".

• The amount of open space in your mouth in the hiss position will vary from approximately the size of a pea (for the 10 blow on a C harp) to the size of a marble (for the 8 blow on a G harp). Vary it, while listening for a sound change or sound disappearance. And when you hear it...

• Blow out hard, so that the air *hisses* out between your tongue hump and the back of your upper front teeth. If your harp weren't in your mouth, you'd feel the air shooting down onto your lower lip and maybe your chin.

• You'll know it when you get it. Blow bending is even more obvious than draw bending. That note just *shoots* down, when you find the right place.

Steps and Half Steps

My digital tuner tells me (in case I don't trust my ear) that 10 blow can be bent both a half step and a whole step position on any harp, at least up to a D. 9 bend can sometimes be bent close to a whole step on some very low harps, but can only be bent a bit more than a half step on higher key harps. As you would expect, on 10 you'll use the "ah-hiss" to get the deepest bend possible (the whole step), and then relax your tongue slightly, which will allow the open space inside your mouth to increase, and the bend to come up to the half step. However, the whole step bend on the 10 blow will usually be the most useful. On 9 blow, you will generally want to use the half step bend (which is good, 'cause the whole step is rarely there!).

8 blow is a funny note. My tuner tells me that I can force some of my harps to bend 8 blow more than a half step, but not an entire whole step. On other harps I can barely get lower than the half step. So I'd call 8 blow bend a half step, which is fine because that provides a much needed high end Blues Scale note.

Once You Get It

After you've gotten any blow note to bend, work on the other two. The start making sure that you can bend each one fully. Go to the scales that use blow bends, and practice them — playing the scales will help you get the proper step or half step from each bend. Read and apply all of the advanced techniques to each blow bend, also. Here are the ones that are most useful when blowing:

• Play the unbent note, bend it, and **slide** from the bend down (blowing).

• **Articulate** your blow bends. Learn to find the "doo" (bent note) position, then play some "doo-wahs". You may find that you can "dwah" a blow bend easier than you can hold down the "doo", so use some "dwahs" and "dwah-dahs". Make "dah" "doo" patterns, too.

• You can use the above articulations on the **9 blow** anywhere during a **Second Position Blues**, and you can use *any* combinations of blow bends during the Subdominants. (Magic Dick does this for long stretches in many of his songs, as does Stevie Wonder in *Boogie On Reggae Woman* and other great songs).

Experiment, and wail! Following are a few of my faves. Here's one similar to some of the licks used in the late, lamented **Jimmy Reed's** First Position masterpiece, *Bright Lights, Big City*.

•	• • • •	•	•	• • • •	•	•	• • • •
8 8	8 8	7	8	10 10	9	9	8 7
B B	*B B♭*	*B*	*B*	*B B♭*	*B*	*B♭*	*B B*

This one illustrates a Second Position use of blow and draw bends, similar to the intro of **J. Geil's** *Whammer Jammer:*

doo wah			*doo*	*wah*	*dah*		*ooooh*
•		• • • • • •	•	•		•	• • • • • •
4 4		<u>56</u>	9	9	10		10
D♭D		*D*	*B♭*	*B*	*B*		*B♭*

And this one illustrates the use of First Position low draw and high blow bends, using a repeated Hoochie Coochie style lick (page 50) with two beats worth of *any* blow bends inserted into the two beats that were silent. Practice the HC, then make up some blow bend inserts!

(• • •)		•		•		•		•
2	3	2	3	4	10	10	9	9
D	D♭	D	D♭	B	B	B♭	B♭	B

The Overblow Bends

Few harp players even know that these "over-blows" exist, and even fewer use them, for good reasons. They're tough, and bad for your reeds (start on an old harp that you don't care much about), but will provide extra usable notes.

To overblow 6, practice blow bending 10, then 9, then 8. Feel how the open space between your tongue and the roof of your mouth is larger with each lower hole. Skip 7, then try to blow bend 6 as though it were just another blow bend. It will take much more air, and a tighter lip seal. On the 4 and 6 blow, the bend raises (yes, raises!) the unbent note by a step and a half. So 4 blow to 4 blow bend = 7 blow to 8 blow bend. And 6 blow to 6 blow bend = 2 draw to 3 draw half step bent. On the 5 blow, it raises the note by a whole step, so 5 blow to 5 blow bend = 2 blow to 2 draw half step bend. Your most useful note of the three is 6 blow bent, as you'll see when you play the High End Second Position Blues Scale (page 62). And try this *wild* rock lick: (Hint: The Bend Tape will really help!)

•	•		•		•	•		•	•		•
6	6	6	5	5	4	3	4	5	6	6
B	B♭	B	D	B	D	D	D	B	B	B♭

Bending The Chromatic

Yes, the chro notes can be bent – some. But do it with caution, because you'll be sorry if you blow a reed on your hundred dollar axe! I recommend only using an "oy" technique on the chro – slurring the note downward for effect but not actually reaching what you would normally consider a bent note. If you listen to Toots Thielemans or Stevie Wonder, you'll hear that they mostly use gentle "oy's" to accent notes. I cover this subject much more thoroughly in my *Instant Chromatic Harmonica: The Blues/Jazz Improvisation Method.*

The Scales

Yes, these are the heart of the matter. Start playing them as soon as you have the necessary bends. Once they begin to feel familiar, **play** with them! Don't feel like you must steadily play each note, in order, solemnly. Swoop both up and down (play them from left to right, *and* from right to left) these scales, using different rhythms and timing patterns. Leave out a note, or add one. Play your way down to a favorite bend, then stay there and wail for a few seconds before continuing down the scale. Learn a full-harp scale, and skip a chunk, sliding from one end to the other. Apply all of the advanced techniques while you play the scales: "doo"s and "dah"s, "dah-oohs" and "doo-wahs", "dwahs", hand warbles, wah-wahs, and slides. There's musical gold in these scales. Don't be afraid to take a risk, and mine it in a new and exciting way!

Low End 2nd Position Blues Scale

2	3	1	1	1	2	2
D	D^b	B	D^b	D	D_b	D

Low End Major Scale

1	1	2	2	2	3	3	4
B	D	B	D_b	D	D_b	D	B

Mid-Range 2nd Position Blues Scale

2	3	4	4	4	5	6
D	D^b	B	D^b	D	D	B

High End 2nd Position Blues Scale

It's missing a note, but do it anyways.

6	6	7	*oy* 8	*oy* 8	9	9
B	B_b	B	D	D	D	B

High-Low 2nd Position Blues Scale

9	10	10	1	1	2	2
B	B_b	B	D^b	D	D_b	D

These scales are hard (especially the chromatic ones! If you have trouble, try the Bend Tape!

High End Major Scale

7	8	8	9	9	10	10	10
B	D	B	D	B	D	B♭	B

High End 1st Position Blues Scale

7	8	9	9	9	10	10
B	B♭	D	B♭	B	B♭	B

Serious Scales

Two Full Chromatic (Piano-type) Scales* (One Hard, One Brutal)

4	4	4	5	5	6	6	6	6	7	7
B	D♭	D	D♭	B♭	B	D♭	B	D	B♭	D

2	2	2	3	3	3	4	4	4	5
B	D♭	D	D♭	B♭	B	D♭	B	D	B♭

6	6	6	7	7	8	8	9	9	10	10	10
D	D♭	B	D	B	B	D	B	D	B	B♭	B

Entire Harp Major Scales

1	1	2	2	3	3	4	4	5	6	6	7	7	8	8	9	9	10	10	1	1	2	2
B	D	B	D♭	D	B	D♭	B	D	B♭	B	D	B	D♭	B	D	B	D♭	B	B♭	B	D♭	D

Entire Harp Blues Scales

2	3	4	4	5	6	6	7	8	9	9	10	10
D	D♭	B	D♭	D	D	B♭	B	D	B♭	B	D♭	D

*Find some skeptic (who plays a *little* harp) and thinks that all the notes on the piano *aren't* on the ten hole harp. Bet that they are. Then play one of these, and collect.

Other Harp Books

Enjoyed this book? Check out some of my others!

Bending: The Cassette (*Now featuring Overblows!*)
This is a 90 minute demonstration of most of the bends and some of the licks in this book, all done on A, C, and F harps. Not a bending pro, yet? This'll help! **$9.95**

Instant Blues Harmonica (*New 9th Edition!*)
If you're either a new harpist or an experienced player who "just learned on his or her own," this easy to use book and 74 min. playalong CD (for C harp) will give you everything you need. 80 page book and CD: **$12.95!**

Music Theory Made Easy for Harp!
Don't understand positions? Never sure which key harp to use when? Stuck in a rut? Let me teach you everything you need to know about music theory for harp, while showing you how to play one harp in 12 different keys. **Hundreds of blues licks and scales for all level harpists!** Optional 90 min. playalong tape (for A harp) gets you jammin' in 1st, 2nd, 3rd, 4th, & 5th positions. 96 page book — a must-have item for all serious players: **$6.95**

How to Play C & W Harmonica
A complete method for beginner to advanced players who like the sound of Charlie McCoy or Clint Black! All the scales, songs, and structures you need to play C & W today! 64 pg. book, 90 min. tape (for C harp): **$12.95**

The Pocket Harmonica Songbook
42 favorite blues, rock, country, folk, & classical tunes notated for harp: some easy for beginners, others challenging to intermediate players. 64 page book: **$5.95**

Three Minutes to Blues Harp Video!
My unique method guarantees that total beginners will play a riff in minutes! Simple blues songs and licks, in styles from Sonny Terry to Little Walter to John Mayall. Video is 73 min., with C harp **$17.95**, video alone: **$12.95** **Kid's Video**: Ages 5-9, 33 min. **$9.95**, with C harp: **$14.95**

Instant Blues/Jazz Chromatic Harp! (*For C Chro*)
It's easier than ten hole, the way I teach it! Little Walter, Stevie, even Toots style! 112 pg book, 90 min. tape: **$19.95**

Our shipping costs have gone sky-high. We were losing money each time we shipped a $10-$15 order. So now, if *you* order more, we'll pay some of the shipping cost!

SORRY! We hated to do this!

Order is:	Under $10	$10-$25	$25-$50	$50+
Ground	$10	$9	$7	$5
3-day	$13	$12	$10	$8
2-Day	$15	$14	$13	$11
Next Day	$25	$24	$23	$22
US Postal	$8	$6	$5	$3
Canada*	$9	$7	$6	$4

*By US Post, other countries please write/email for charges.